Unspoken Melodies of the Heart

Poetry of Our Times

By Stephen Perez

ISBN: 978-1-962363-71-6 (sc)
ISBN: 978-1-962363-72-3 (e)

Rev. date: 02/28/2024

Contents

My Heart is Yours
This love poem is dedicated to Norma

I give you my heart to keep forever,
I am hoping that you will join it with yours,
So that they can grow together.

It is full of emotions and feelings for you,
That is how I know that you
Will be in my heart forever.

I would do whatever it takes to make you happy.
Your hopes and dreams, I will work to make them
come true.

I don't deserve a lady as special as you, but that
doesn't change my decision.
I have never felt about anyone, the way that I feel
about you.

I hope that I am not out of line, when I say having
you in my life would mean the world.

Saying that I care about you is an understatement.
When they made you, they broke the mold.

A Broken Heart

Although I said I would take the pain,
I didn't realize how hard it would be.

You are always on my mind,
Not a day goes by that your memory doesn't affect
me. '

I miss you every waking moment,
I just can't get used to the idea of us being apart.

Answer me one question...
How am I supposed to go on with this broken heart?

The Love I Want

The love I want is like no other.
The kind that when you're in it, you never want
to leave.
The Kind that leaves you breathless.
Life-changing, and it makes you the kind of person
you want to be.

The love I want is special.
The kind that makes your heart want to explode
with happiness.
The kind people talk about.
You always want to be with that person, and you
can never get enough.

The love I want is hard to find.
If you find the right person, it can make your life
so easy.
The kind that makes your life complete.
The kind that takes it from me, to *we*.

In Love with a Memory

I am in love with a memory, and
I do not know what to do.
Every time I close my eyes, you
are right in front of me.

They say that in time you will forget,
and everything will be fine.
It has been a while since you have gone,
and still, you are deep within me.

Your face and your voice are
etched into my heart.
I try to get over you, but my
heart just will not let go.

So, I am in love with a memory
and there is nothing I can do.
If you know how to get past a memory,
please be sure and let me know.

Forever

Forever-that's how long I want you in my life. That way, my life will be complete.

Forever-that's how long I want you in my arms. That would make my life so sweet.

Forever-that's how long my love for you will last. My love for you will never fade.

Forever-that's how long I will work to make your dreams come true. Just wait and see, all these plans I have made.

At Odds with My Heart

My heart will not accept that you will not have it.
It is fighting me tooth and nail.

It does not understand that you are not interested.
I tell it over and over, to no avail.

It has you on a pedestal, way up high.
To my heart, you are the center of the universe.

It is affecting my health.
If it continues, I may need a nurse.

It lives in its own little world of make-believe.
It will not see the truth, not even a bit.

But the truth is, the two of us just were not a fit.

It's Not Your Fault

It's not your fault that I walk around like a zombie.
Not knowing what hour or day it is.

It's not your fault that I can't stop thinking about you.
Always feeling like there is something amiss.

It's not your fault that I love you so much it hurts.
Seeing you every day and not being able to touch you.

It's not your fault that I can't think straight.
Walking around, not knowing what to do.

It's my fault for being so shy.
That I can't tell you how I feel; for being afraid of being rejected.

It's my fault that my feelings for you are so strong.
It makes me feel like all my senses are being tested.

When You're in Love

When you're in love, everything seems better.
It makes everything in life feel sweeter.

When you're in love, it makes your disposition
seem brighter.
It makes everyone around you seem friendlier.

When you're in love, it seems like you're walking
on air.
It makes you feel ten feet tall.

When you're in love, whatever life throws at you,
you can do no wrong.
It doesn't matter what it is, you can handle it all.

You're There

I wake up in the morning and you're there.
Every morning, I wake up and you're the first thing
on my mind.

I go through the trials of the day, and you're there.
When I am having a hard day, there is only one
cure that I can find.

I get ready to wind down and go to bed, and you're
there.
As I think back on the day I've had, you dominate
the time.

Not a day goes by that I don't think about you,
and you're always there.
Maybe it's just me, but I take it as a sign.

My Ray of Sunshine

There is a black cloud hanging over my head.
The day is starting off badly.

All the trials and tribulations of the day are starting
to add up.
They are getting to be too much, it's all that I can
stand.

I see you walk in, and all my worries just melt away.
As crazy as life can get, bring it on because I won't
mind.

In all the darkness that exists in this world, you
bring me happiness.
You are my little ray of sunshine.

Your Smile

Your smile is contagious, it makes me light up.
It's all that I need to brighten my day.

When I've had a bad day and I'm feeling down,
Your smile makes the sun shine.
It washes all my worries away.

To see you smile means the world to me,
There is nothing I wouldn't do to make it shine.

Whenever I see you, there is that smile.
It makes me happy every time.

Your Beauty

The first time I saw you, I could not believe my eyes. Your beauty took my breath away.

Your smile always lifts my spirits. I love your laugh; it makes my day.

You are an amazing lady. You make my heart overflow with emotion. I can hardly contain myself.

Each day I see you, my heart just seems to light up. All my stress and worries just seem to dissolve.

I count my blessings every day, glad that you came into my life.
I can't imagine you not being there.

My days seem to be better and brighter; being around you makes it seem like I am always walking on air.

My Love

My love for you comes from the deepest recesses
of my heart.
What I feel for you, I have never felt before.

Every time I see you, it always makes me smile.
You wake all my senses and leave me wanting more.

I can never get enough of you,
I am like a junkie looking for drugs.

You always leave me looking for your love,
Dreaming that one day I'll have your kisses and
hugs.

You make me feel like the luckiest man alive.
Having you in my life would be the icing on the
cake.

I can't get you out of my mind.
I think of you every moment that I'm awake.

Cupid's Arrow

Cupid shoots his arrow and
down goes another heart.

Two hearts become one.

Your eyes glaze over, you're breathing
fast, you start to sweat.

The love bug has bitten.

When the love bug bites, your entire
world is turned upside down.

You will never be the same.

There are many lovers' games that can
be played, and they can all be fun.

But when two hearts are involved,
it's a whole new ball game.

What the Heart Wants

I tell my heart that you don't want me,
You're not ready for a relationship.

It does not listen-the heart wants what the heart
wants.

I tell my heart that you're not into me, it really
will not work.
My heart just will not have it-the heart wants
what the heart wants.

I tell my heart that I just want to be happy, but
it keeps going back to you.
I have no answer-the heart wants what the heart
wants.

I tell my heart it must get over you,
I don't stand a chance-the heart wants what the
heart wants.

The heart is always right.
It can never be wrong because the heart just wants
what the heart wants.

A Welcome Invasion

You have invaded my mind.
You're the first thing I think of when I wake up.

You have invaded my thoughts and dreams.
You're the last thing I think about when I go to bed.

You have invaded my heart, my love for you is
boundless and unending.
My heart is overflowing with love for you.

You have invaded my whole being.
You are the center of my universe and my love for
you will always be true.

Letter to My Grandson

Although I did not get to know you when you first came into the world, I knew that you would be special.

There is not a day that you do not amaze me. When I look at you, I can see your mind working with all the wonder and gleaming of someone with lots of questions.

As I watch you grow, I am in awe of the things that you say and do. You are an old soul in a little boy's body.

One day, you will amaze and dazzle the world, just as you do me.

I can't wait.

I love you,
Paw Paw

Keep the Fire Burning

When you both met, there were sparks.

You both felt something that you had never felt before.

Although you did not know what it was, it made you feel warm inside.

You did not want the feeling to stop; you kept coming back for more.

Now that time has moved on and so have those feelings.

You find it hard to keep your heart beating.

Dig deep down into your heart and show her that you still love her.

That there is nothing that will keep the old flame from burning.

Ler her know that you still live for her.

That your world revolves around her.

Let her know that there is no one as special as her, no one that can make your life better like she can.

Christmas Without You

Dedicated in memory of my daughter

You were only with me a few days, and yet you were not.

I hope that you felt the love that we had for you.

Your dreams and wishes would never be realized; all the things the world had for you.

All the holidays that you would miss, with the people that loved you so much.

Somehow, you were not meant to be with us for very long, there were other plans for you.

As much as you are missed, I know that one day I will see you again!

One day we will be together.

That day will be Heaven to me. Finally, being with my daughter will be so nice-no feeling would be better.

She'll Be There

You wake up at 2 AM in your crib
because you're hungry.
You start crying to get your mother's attention.
She'll be there.

You're playing outside and you fall and
skin your knee and get a boo-boo.
You cry out to mom for help.
She'll be there.

You graduate from high school
with all your friends.
You wonder and think about
what your future will be.
She'll be there.

As you travel down the highway of life,
there will always be bumps in the road.
You look around for someone to help.
No need-just look in your rearview mirror.
She'll be there.

Thank you, mom.

This Woman

This woman will be your biggest
critic and yet, your best friend.

This woman will fight for you tooth and nail.
She'll give you all she has till the very end.

This woman will be beside you through thick
and thin. She'll love you forever and ever.

This woman will put you above everything
and everyone else, including herself.

Who is this woman?

Your mother.

The Loneliest Sound in America

We pay tribute to the heroes that are
chosen to defend our freedom.

We set aside a special day.

We honor them with activities and parades.

We understand and are grateful for
the heavy price that was paid.

When all our veterans have left this world, they
are laid to rest in a special place called Arlington.

They are given a special goodbye with a
thirty-one gun salute, a flag, and taps,
this is the loneliest sound in America.

Angels in a Foreign Land

They are chosen to defend our way of life; they gladly go in harm's way.

They are in a land that they do not know. There is a heavy debt that they could pay.

Some will come home, and some will not. That is the sad truth.

They do what they do so we can enjoy our way of life. Freedom for me and you.

These are our sons and daughters, and it's hard to let them go.

But they want to go and don't think twice.

From every American, thank you for your sacrifice.

IT

Like a thief in the night, it comes and takes,
Our jobs, our loved ones, and our livelihood.

It lingers like a nasty fog, and it won't go away;
making it hard to acquire necessities like toiletries,
fuel, and food.

It makes us prisoners in our own homes-we lock
down and become hostages to it.

The children can't go outside or go to school. Most
are too young, they don't know what is going on.
They don't understand it.

The experts are working hard to stop it. They tell
us to wear masks and keep everything clean.

The world as we know it has been turned upside
down. For all this hardship and trouble, we can
thank Covid-19.

A Silent Enemy

400,000 souls gone, but not forgotten.

Fathers, mothers, sisters, and brothers-the world is under siege by an invisible foe.

2020 has been a difficult year, one that will not soon be forgotten,

The medical community is hard at work, and finally has something to show.

The nation still has a long journey ahead. A road full of uncertainty, but some vaccines have been made available.

Delivery of the vaccines is a slow process, so many people and so little time.

It will be difficult, but with all our resources, success is inevitable.

Freedom in Peril

Freedom, right now, is the most expensive commodity in the world.

But at the same time, it has come to unite the people of all countries.

Many people around the world will suffer the cost of freedom, but not so much as the people of Ukraine.

They will fight till their last breath to keep their country free.

The people of the world will not tolerate the forceful invasion of any country.

The Soviet Union has come to know this as truth.

The people of the world have let their voices be heard.

The battle for peace and freedom will not be easy.

But for the world to coexist in the future, this is what we will need to do.

Stand united.